The Port of Ayr

A Pictorial History

by

James M. Moore

The Common Seal of the Royal Burgh of Ayr

Preface and Acknowledgements

Having been brought up in Glasgow, I had acquired an interest in the Clyde and its shipping, but I knew little of Ayr until I arrived here in 1966.
My enthusiasm for this area grew rapidly and there must have been something in the genes, as I have since discovered that my great great grand-father lived and worked in Ayr, in the 1820's.

I should like to express my gratitude to all who have helped in this production. Firstly the staff of the Carnegie Library; in particular Sheena Andrew and Sheila West.
For old photographs, I must mention my late friends Bob Pepper, Alfred T. Scott and Bill Williams. Help in this line also came from John McCallum and Hugh Anderson of Ayr Photographic Society, Peter Lockhart, John Innes and James McMeikan.

I am indebted to many past and present members of Associated British Ports' staff, especially Captain Newton Brown and the late Alec Wills, Harbour Foreman, for much valuable information. I must thank C & G Print, Troon for their guidance and unfailing friendly co-operation throughout. Thanks are also due to my wife for her help with proof reading and ready assistance in many other ways. Finally, it is a pleasure to acknowledge financial support for this publication from the Strathmartine Trust, Edinburgh.

James M. Moore
Ayr
September 2005

Published by Portland Press, Troon
ISBN 0 9528771 47

Ayr is the oldest port on the west coast of Scotland and in the country as a whole, giving precedence only to Leith and Dundee. It was granted its first Royal Charter in 1205 by William the Lion.

The type of Roman ship which might possibly have been built at Ayr. However, John Strawhorn emphasised that there was no conclusive proof that the Romans occupied Ayr.
At any rate, the illustration shows a ship about to come in on the PORT side and on the other side is the "steerboard", STARBOARD.

Types of ship built at Ayr in the 13th century for the Scottish Navy on the order of Alexander III.

(Illustrations from "Contributions to Scottish Maritime History" by John Crighton Jnr.)

Ayr Harbour.

CHRONOLOGICAL SUMMARY OF EVENTS.

Date.
A.D.

836	Landing of Alpin.
1197	Building of the New Castle by William the Lion.
1202	Charter of William the Lion.
1236	Charters of Alexander II.
1261	Charter of Alexander III.
1263	Coming of Haco of Norway. Battle of Largs.
1315	Edward Bruce sails for Ireland.
Circa 1320	The Ayr Manuscript.
1471	Act for encouragement of Shipbuilding. (Also 1493, 1503).
1490	Precept of James IV. regarding purchase of fish by foreigners at " free Burghs."
1497	Perkin Warbeck embarks for Ireland.
1513	Scottish Fleet under Arran at Ayr.
1515	Regent Albany arrives at Ayr.
1528	Earliest record of coal working in Barony of Alloway.
1580	Founding of Mariners' Society.
1587	Royal Commission on state of Harbour.
1588	Grant of Imposts by James VI. for upkeep of Harbour.
1588	Shipwrecked Sailors of Armada given hospitality.
1590	Action against the Pirates.
1593	Ban on Export of Coal.
1599 and 1604	" Stents " for the " bigging of the key."
1602	Vessels in Quarantine to prevent spread of Plague.
1610	Address of Magistrates to James VI.

By Hugh McGhee, from the Proceedings of the
Ayrshire Archaeological and Natural History Society.

EXPLANATORY NOTES

In 1513 the Scottish Fleet under the Earl of Arran at Ayr consisted of 16 great vessels and 10 smaller craft.

1580   The Mariners' Society for the Welfare of Seamen was in fact started to help sailors, and their dependants, who had suffered at the hands of the pirates. The Statistical Account states "For the benefit of decayed mariners".

1588   Shipwrecked sailors of the Armada given hospitality. A war was in progress between Elizabeth I of England and King Philip II of Spain, but this was before the Union of the Crowns and Scotland was a neutral country. Robert Maxwell, the Treasurer of the Burgh, spent £4.00 of the town's money "for meat and drink to the pure Spainyardis"; also £1.00 for shoes and £4.00 for lodgings.

1590   Action against the pirates. They tended to lie in wait for shipping between Ailsa Craig and the south end of Arran.

1602   Vessels in Quarantine to prevent the spread of Plague. This would be Bubonic Plague, spread by the black rat, through a type of flea which also affects humans. The Black Death was an example of this condition in the 14th Century.

Air from the East, 1693, from Captain John Slezer's Theatrum Scotiae. On the right in the background is Cromwell's Citadel (1652-54) and the Church of St. John the Baptist.

The premises of Alexander Oliphant (1766)
(See text on page 4)

ARRIVALS/SAILINGS BOOK OF AYR HARBOUR

This refers to the year 1774, the time of Burns. Some years ago it was rescued from a bonfire by the Harbour Foreman, the late Alec Wills.

The vessels were brigs, sloops, boats and whirries. Many of the names were double-barrelled eg. *Fortunate Mally*, *George and Bella*. The ships belonged to Ayr, other ports on the Clyde, Ireland, the Isle of Man and the Solway. They had arrived from local ports but many had come from Ireland, one from Liverpool and one from Easdale with slates. The majority were bringing in limestone for the numerous iron works in the area.

On 9th June the Brig *Buck*, Master James Wilson, had arrived from Portugal with a cargo of wine. This ship of 50 tons was owned by Alexander Oliphant & Co. who had had her built in 1767 by an Ayr shipbuilder, John Fraser, at a cost of £600. The company had started business in 1766 and was a fore-runner of Whighams, now Corney and Barrow, which is going strong today in the same premises in Academy Street. *Buck* took about 16 days from Lisbon to Ayr.

John Strawhorn in "The History of Ayr" mentions that, in1765, the Crown took control over the Isle of Man from where many smugglers had previously operated. A number of such merchants now found it convenient to transfer from Douglas to Ayr, including Alexander Oliphant and they seemed to be able to conduct a happy combination of ordinary trade and smuggling. Oliphant had agents in Madeira, Cadiz, Lisbon, Oporto, Barcelona, Bordeaux and Guernsey; he had cellars in Ayr, Kilmarnock, Moffat and Stranraer and customers from the north of England to the West Indies.

Certainly in 1774 Ayr Harbour was very busy; on 1st June ten ships came in and over the first nine days of the month twenty seven ships arrived. The main export was coal and also some timber, with occasional cargoes of soap, salt, sugar and general goods.

4

Day of the Month 1774	Rigg	Vessels Names	Master's Names	Place they Belong too	Place they Came from
June 1st	Brig	Fortunate Mally	William M'Kie	Ayr	Newry
..	Sloop	Ann	James Miller	Greenock	Larne
..	..	Charming Mally	Alexander Stewart	Larne	..
..	..	Freemason	John M'wattie	Portglasgow	Larne
..	Boat	Success	John Simpson	Ayr	Stranraer
..	Sloop	Jeanie & Peggy	John Seat	Bangor	Larne
..	..	Nancy	Clowd Lang	Greenock	Larne
..	..	James	John Crumley	Larne	..
..	Brig	Peggy & Polly	Henry Worklaw	Portferry	Larne
..	Whirrie	Eulain	Charles Crawford	Portferry	Larne
2	Boat	Whale	Robert Dick	Girvan	..
3	Brig	Two Batchelors	John Caldwell	Larne	..
..	Sloop	Mary & Betty	Patrick While	Newry	Larne
..	..	Martha	John Hughs	Newry	Larne
..	..	Nancy	Ross Brown	Newry	Larne
..	Whirrie	John & Betty	John Cottrop	Killoch	..
4th	Sloop	George & Bella	William Cowley	Isle of Man	Liverpool
..	..	Clanbrissill	William Bryace	Dundalk	..
5th	..	Mally	John M'dowall	Ayr	Esdale
..	Boat	Endeavour	Andrew M'indlie	Ayr	Irvin
7th	Sloop	Oria	John Rowen	Dundrum	..
..	..	Frances	James Rowen	Killoch	Larne
8th	..	John & Thomas	John Gown	Isle of Man	..
..	..	Isabella	Alexander M'millen	Campbellton	Wexford
..	..	Herring	Robert Kean	Isle of Man	..
9th	Brig	Buck	James Wilson	Ayr	Portopart
..	Sloop	Mary	Eldred Burnet	Workington	..

This notice is from the Air Advertiser of 6th July 1815 and describes the arrival at Ayr of the fourth Clyde Steamer, *P.S. Glasgow* on 1st July. This was the first steamer to call at the town.

On Saturday last, the Glasgow Steam Boat, which left that City in the morning, later stopping at several places, arrived here at 9 o'clock in the evening, with a great number of passenger. She came in in fine stile, against wind and tide, and her arrival was greeted by a great number of spectators. She sailed again on Monday morning at 8 o'clock for Troon, and intended to call at Ardrossan, &c. on her way back to Glasgow, which she was expected to reach that evening.

John Cockburn—S. MEDAL.
The Number of Students, who have attended the Academy since last September, is 538.

☞ The Classes are to meet again on Monday the 11th of September.

The Glasgow Steam Boat

SAILS from AIR on Friday first, at nine o'clock morning, and calls at TROON, IRVINE, ARDROSSAN, LARGS, and all the Towns on the Coast to Glasgow.
AIR, 2d Aug. 1815.

TO BE SOLD,

by Public Roup, within the House possessed by the late JOHN HUNTER, Hardware Merchant in Air,

The Steam Boat sailing advert from the Air Advertiser of 3rd August 1815.

This painting by Alexander Nasmyth, illustrates the worst disaster in the annals of the Clyde steamers. In darkness in the early morning of 21st October 1825, Henry Bell's second *Comet*, on a voyage from Inverness to Glasgow, collided with the steamer *Ayr* travelling down firth past Gourock. *Comet* sank in a few minutes but *Ayr* managed to reach Greenock. The death toll was about seventy and Thomas McClelland, the master of *Ayr*, was criticised for leaving the scene, but his own ship was only kept afloat with great difficulty. A public inquiry was held but despite Captain McClelland's exoneration, he emigrated soon after.

NIMROD (1834)

Nimrod sailed from Glasgow to Greenock, Largs, Millport and Ayr.

ELEGANT NEW STEAM-PACKET
BETWEEN AIR AND GLASGOW.

IN consequence of the Air Steamer, COUNTESS of GLASGOW, having been Sold, the Public are respectfully informed that the New, Elegant and remarkably swift sailing Steam-Packet,

NIMROD,

Neil Currie, Commander,

Commenced plying between AIR and GLASGOW yesterday; and will leave Glasgow on Friday at Half-past 9 o'clock, morning, and Air on Saturday at Half-past 7 o'clock, morning, and will continue to leave Air for Greenock and Glasgow, calling at the intermediate Ports, on Tuesdays, Thursdays, and Saturdays, returning from Glasgow to Air, by the same route, on Mondays, Wednesdays, and Fridays leaving Glasgow at Half-past 9 o'clock morning.

The Nimrod is fitted-up with capacious Holds, for carrying Goods under Hatches.   Goods shipped

An advert from the "Air Advertiser"
19th June 1834.

A Burns' Festival was held on the banks of the Doon on 6th August 1844, in honour of the genius of the poet and to welcome his three surviving sons. Everyone of any importance was there and the attendance was between 70,000 and 100,000. There were apologies from Thomas Moore, Thomas Carlyle and William Wordsworth, Poet Laureate. Among the 184 stewards was Sir Thomas Brisbane, who had been one of Wellington's Generals; he became Governor of New South Wales and gave his name to Brisbane, the capital of Queensland. His home was Brisbane House behind Largs.

BURNS'S FESTIVAL.

THE Splendid New Steamer, LADY BRIS-BANE, John Gilmour, Commander, will Sail from STRANRAER on the Morning of the GRAND FESTIVAL, Tuesday 6th August, at 5 o'Clock, morning, and from GIRVAN at 7 o'Clock, thus affording an hour's leisure in Ayr, previous to the arrangement of the Grand Procession in the Low Green.

The Steamer will remain in Ayr until the whole of the Festivities are concluded, and will start on her return at 7 o'Clock evening.

The Proprietors of the BRISBANE have resolved, on this Great National Festival occasion, to give their Friends and the Public a Benefit.

Fares, Going and Returning :

Cabin, from and to Stranraer,	5s. 0d
Steerage, do. do.	3s. 0d
Cabin, from and to Girvan,	2s. 0d
Steerage, do. do.	1s. 6d.

The LADY BRISBANE will leave STRAN-RAER for the GREAT AGRICULTURAL MEETING *at* GLASGOW on Wednesday the 7th, Thursday 8th, and Friday 9th August, at 4 o'Clock Morning, *precisely*, in order to be in time for the 8 o'Clock Morning Train from Ayr to Glasgow ; and will remain in Ayr, on each of *the* above days, until the arrival of the Half-past 6 o'Clock down Train from Glasgow.

Ayr, 29th July, 1844.

Advert for *Lady Brisbane* Festival Sailings.

LADY BRISBANE (1842)

Lady Brisbane sailed between Largs, Millport and Ayr and played an important part in the Burns' Festival.

SCOTIA (1845)

Scotia of the Glasgow and Stranraer Steam Packet Co., was one of the vessels, along with *Briton,* which escorted Sir John Ross's Arctic Expedition down firth in 1850. Both vessels were normally on the Ayr - Campbeltown run at that time. The illustration shows the ship in Girvan.

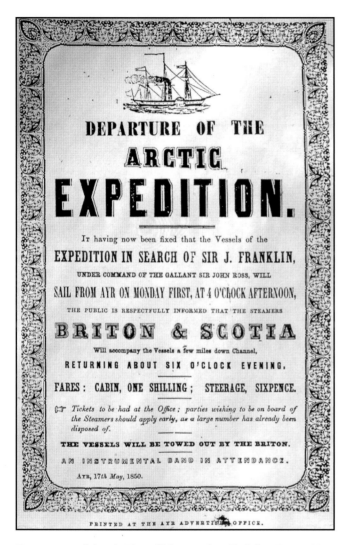

Departure of Arctic Expedition under Sir John Ross, May 1850, in search of his friend Sir John Franklin. His ship, *Felix*, had been built for him in the north harbour, Ayr by Sloan and Gemmel.

Sir John Ross

A vigorous, fiery, red-haired Scot who was educated at Ayr Academy and was in command of the Swedish Navy at the age of thirty one. In later years he had built, for his residence, what is now the North West Castle Hotel in Stranraer.

Fittings in the windows of the front lounge there still showed evidence, until a few years ago, of where he would use his telescope for the inspection of shipping in the bay.

At the time of his departure on this expedition, he was said to be 73 years of age.

What had happened was that an Ayr schoolboy had seen an unusual gull, swimming around outside the Yacht Club, It was confirmed that this was a Ross's Gull and within a few hours enthusiasts were arriving from all over the country. This was the first sighting of the bird in Ayrshire and probably only the second on the Scottish mainland.

Ross's Gull

A small Arctic gull about the size of a black-headed gull, with a pinkish breast and a wedge-shaped tail. The adult is shown in the centre of the picture. The gull was first described by Sir James Clark Ross, the nephew of Sir John and an equally famous polar explorer; rather odd that it should turn up a few hundred yards from where Sir John went to school.

Ayr Harbour, by J.C. Oldmeadow, circa 1850

The Ratton Quay

The Ratton Quay, mentioned by Burns in "The Brigs of Ayr" viz. "And from Glenbuck down to the Ratton-Key Auld Ayr is just one lengthen'd tumbling sea -" This was probably taken in the early 1850's and must be one of the first photographs of Ayr harbour. The sailing vessels on the left are at the quay, quite obviously inset from the river; the line of the quay wall was altered to its present straighter form in 1855.

Ayr, from the Shipyard North Quay 1859

This is one of an excellent series of photographs taken by Fisher Mack, a local photographer.

Fisher Mack

Andrew McIlwraith

Andrew McIlwraith came from an old Ayrshire family which owned Content House, where the Fire Station now stands. In the 1860's, with his two brothers and father he started a shipping company, the Scottish Line, trading from Ayr and Glasgow and eventually, London, Melbourne and Brisbane. The headquarters moved to London and in 1875 Andrew teamed up with Malcolm McEacharn from Islay to form McIlwraith McEacharn, and this firm is still going strong today, with headquarters in Sydney; the House Flag is the Lion Rampant.

McILWRAITH McEACHARN LIMITED A.C.N. 004 130 438

Incorporated in Victoria
Head Office: 32 Walker Street, North Sydney, N.S.W. 2060
Please address correspondence to: P.O. Box 83, North Sydney 2059
Telephone: 956 4000. Telex: 178116. Fax: 954 1445
Cables & Telegrams: "Coomera", Sydney

In 1879, with the steamer *Strathleven*, they successfully brought back the first refrigerated cargo of meat and butter from Australia.

Andrew McIlwraith became one of the greatest benefactors of Ayr County Hospital and gave his name to the McIlwraith Ward.

CONTENT HOUSE
The McIlwraith family home.

This illustration came from the Historical Museum in St. George's, Bermuda. The explanation is that, due to the American Civil War and the blockade of the southern ports, fast ships of shallow draught were much in demand by the Confederate forces. Acquiring these was politically difficult and the bills of sale were often made out to mythical personages, such as the "Emperor of China". *Caledonia* was sold and left the Clyde on Christmas Day, 1863, for Bermuda with her windows boarded up and her alleyways stacked with coal, crossing the Atlantic without difficulty.

The "Caledonia"
From Glasgow to Bermuda. Put into Cork December 20th and sailed December 31st 1863

CALEDONIA (1844)
Ayr Steamer of 1863.

BONNIE DOON I (1870)

This vessel provided summer excursion sailings. She had been built by T. B. Seath of Rutherglen shipyard, who was also part - owner along with Thomas Steele of Ayr.

SPECIAL AND SELECT EXCURSION
TO
AILSA CRAIG,
On *THURSDAY NEXT,* 2nd *JULY,*
Allowing Passengers Two Hours on the CRAIG, by permission of Lord Ailsa,

PER FINE SWIFT   SALOON STEAMER,

"BONNIE DOON"
(Weather favourable and casualties excepted),
Sailing from AYR at 11.15 A.M. ; arriving back about 5 P.M.

RETURN FARES............Saloon, 2s 6d ; Steerage, 2s.

EXCURSION (SAME EVENING)

BONNIE DOON II (1876)

It was unusual for a steamer to provide a landing cruise to Ailsa Craig. She was a fine vessel but, unfortunately she had her mechanical problems and became known as "Bonnie Breakdoon".

14

BONNIE DOON II
Land O' Burns Poster.

The Funnel and Flag of the Ayr Steam Shipping Company (1876)

This company had a large cargo trade in the days when the blast furnaces of Ayrshire were working to full capacity. The vessels brought in iron ore and limestone and took out coal and pig-iron. The company was controlled by the Laird Line from 1908.

S.S. Dunure (ex *Cedar*, 1878) was acquired by the company in 1906 and was typical of their vessels. From 1908 she was on the Ayr - Belfast run. Eventually she went to Greece and was broken up in 1938.

In the background is the Trades Hotel in York Street, which was severely damaged by fire some years ago and later became Chalenvale House Training Centre.

The company had 13 ships and they certainly were unlucky; no fewer than 8 of them were lost.

S.S. DUNURE

The South Pier before widening

This photograph, in the late 1870's, also shows
Barracks on the right. The pier was eventually broad
by the addition of a wooden structure on the north
and wood was replaced by concrete around 1
However the newer portion has never had the same
foundation as the original part, and could becon
source of difficulty.

Paddle Tug AYR II (1878)

She cost £4,000 and was fitted with Disconnecting
Engines; this allowed the paddle wheels to rotate in
opposite directions with a great increase in
manoeuvrability. She sank after a collision in Ayr
Bay in 1890.

On the North Quay, behind the tug, the old Pilot
House is clearly seen.

Provost Thomas Steele

Thomas Steele was Provost of Ayr from 1876 until 1882 and was also President of the Ayr Harbour Trust. Previously he had been Managing Director of Troon Shipbuilding Co., before the yard was acquired by the Ailsa company. At one time he had owned a considerable fleet of sailing ships and steamers as well, some of which got as far as Japan. He was a partner in Seath and Steele which operated the "Land O' Burns" summer excursion sailings from Glasgow to Ayr. He was also a grain merchant with premises at 39 South Quay.

Under his guidance the Wet Dock was constructed in the North Harbour, the north end of the esplanade was completed, and a Slip Dock was built in the new shipyard in the South Harbour. A pedestrian swing bridge crossed the entrance to the dock and on it was a plaque stating that it had been presented to the people of Ayr by Provost Steele. It provided for a popular walk along the esplanade to the South Pier, over the bridge, and then up the south side of the river to the centre of the town.

Provost Steele's house in Montgomerie Terrace

The Swing-Bridge across the Slip-Dock

This was much appreciated by the local boys.

He had steps built down from his back garden, to give him direct access to his grain store below and the harbour. Thomas Steele died in 1915, aged 89, a great benefactor of the town.

NEW SHIPYARD

Sloan and Gemmel's shipyard, on the north side of the river, had built wooden - hulled vessels only. They were well - known for producing fast sailing clippers. The yard moved to the south side in 1881, under McKnight, McCredie & Co., and from 1884 until 1902 was run by Samuel McKnight & Co., until taken over by the Ailsa Shipbuilding Co. They built 64 ships, such as paddle steamers and coasters, with hulls of iron and then steel.

Samuel McKnight's House

He "lived above the shop" in Seabank Road, just about as near as one could get to the shipyard.

Painting by John Nicholson

MADGE WILDFIRE (1886)

Advert from Ayr
Observer, 1887.

Captain Robert Campbell ordered this vessel from Samuel McKnight & Co., Ayr. Apparently she was in service just four months after the signing of the contract.

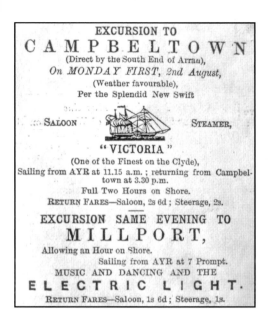

From the Ayrshire Post 30 July 1886.

VICTORIA (1886)

This ship owned by Gillies and Campbell, was the first Clyde steamer to be fitted with electric light.

P.S. NEPTUNE (1892)

A Valentine postcard of the Glasgow and South Western Railway ship, entering Ayr Harbour. You'll note the message along the foot *"Juno* is the name of this steamer" - a pardonable error. The post-mark was 20th July 1904, (the Glasgow Fair). It was sent by a lady with the name of Jean, who stated that the weather was "spiffing", and her holiday address was York Street, Ayr.

Ayr Pier   Valentines Series

Juno is the name of this steamer

Taken in the mid-eighteen nineties, the tug is *Ben Ledi* with the funnels mounted athwartships.

Captain Donald McTavish

The first skipper of the *Juno*. He was the only bachelor in the fleet and this regularly resulted in a bevy of young ladies, at the end of the pier, to wave him off.

P.S. JUNO (1898) on Trials

P.S. JUNO (1898)

With this ship the Glasgow and South Western Railway really tightened their grip on the Ayr summer excursion sailings. She was built by the Clydebank Engineering and Shipbuilding Co. Ltd. and initially had been intended for cross-channel work; she was a big solid ship and was ideally suited to cruising in the open waters of the lower firth. Her success was such that she continued to sail from Ayr for 33 years.

Juno leaving Ayr, and *Waverley* (1899), lost at Dunkirk in 1940, berthed at the South Pier. The young ladies on the right may well have been down to wave Captain McTavish off.

Juno leaving for an Evening Cruise.

The Insignia on the Station Hotel,
Ayr, of the G. & S.W.R., also known
as the "Good and Safe Wee Railway".

G. & S.W.R. War Memorial on Platform 3, Ayr Station.
This was transferred from St. Enoch Station, Glasgow, when it was demolished in 1966.

This was part of a fine collection of lantern slides taken by a well-known Ayr architect, James A. Morris. The vessel is likely to be *Garnock* or *Burnock* in the 1890's, built by McKnight. Note the forest of sailing ship masts in the background.

"Disabled", taken by John Pratt, a local photographer in the early twentieth century.

Advert for Ayr Steam Shipping Company from Ayr Directory of 1910-11.

The illustration is maybe overdoing it, as their vessels had no more than a single funnel and two masts!

It is interesting that the departures from the other end are given in Irish Time.

It seems that, until March 1916, Irish Time was 25 minutes behind Greenwich Mean Time.

Telegrams—"M'QUISTON, AYR."   Telephone No. 89.

Ayr Steam Shipping Coy., Ltd.

SCOTLAND and IRELAND.

REGULAR STEAM COMMUNICATION WITH
BELFAST and LARNE via AYR.

Ayr to Belfast Daily (Sundays excepted) at Midnight.
Belfast to Ayr Daily (Sundays excepted) at 8 p.m. (Irish).
Ayr to Larne Every Monday, Wednesday, and Friday, 12 Night.
Larne to Ayr Every Tuesday, Thursday, 8 p.m.; Saturday at or after 6 p.m. (Irish time).

Regular Service between AYR and CAMPBELTOWN.

For Fares, &c., apply to

Ayr Steam Shipping Coy., Limited, Ayr.

"Low Tide", also by John Pratt. The vessel, *Orion* was having maintenance work done, on the gravel bank.

"Harbour Ayr". An attractive post-card produced by a German company about 1910. On the left north side, is the dredger *Kyle* (1885 - 1938) and further up is a Laird Line ship, either *Azalea* or *Dunure*. On the south side is *Ailsa* of Leith unloading timber. This was often partly unloaded into the river, and was towed upstream and across the river, to Alexander's Sawmills' original site near the Victoria Bridge.

HARBOUR, AYR.

The launch of the second lifeboat named *Janet Hoyle* in 1910, from the slip at the Compass Pier.

"Harbour from Town Hall, Ayr"

A Valentine postcard of 1913. Provan's Temperance Hotel is obvious, on the corner of Fort Street and South Harbour Street. On the right, the railway bridge to the south harbour is seen and, above it, is the Fishermen's Dock.

Aerial view of the harbour in the 1920's. A Laird Line ship is lying in the river on the north quay wall. The shipyard is shown at the bottom right corner, with the swing bridge leading to the South Pier and the end of the prom. Note all the little plumes of smoke --

"When Coal and Steam Ruled"

26

VILLE DE PAPEETE
14th November 1928

One of the last ships launched from the shipyard, then owned by the Ailsa Shipbuilding Company. She was built for a French company for service in the Pacific.
(Papeete is the capital of Tahiti)

Ville de Papeete on trials.

S.S. CANTABRIA
Santander, Northern Spain

She had discharged iron ore at Ardrossan and was coming to Ayr, light, in a gale on 23rd November 1928, to load coal. The Ayr pilot, William McCallum, had to board the ship by means of a tug requisitioned from Troon; the vessel dragged her anchor and was driven ashore near the Pavilion on the promenade. She was eventually refloated on 29th January 1929.

Cartoon from the Ayrshire Post, 7/12/28

Cantabria had become a popular tourist attraction. During the Spanish Civil War she was sunk off Cromer, in November 1938, by a ship of General Franco's Insurgent Navy called *Nadir*, which naturally caused a lot of political excitement.

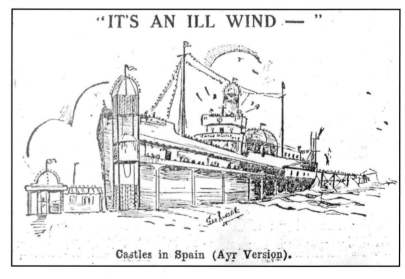

"IT'S AN ILL WIND — "

Castles in Spain (Ayr Version).

P.S. JUNO Sailings leaflet of 1930

She is now in the colours of the London, Midland and Scottish Railway Co..

South Harbour, Ayr

A calm Sunday morning in 1931, with *Juno* and *Glen Sannox*.
Juno was withdrawn at the end of that season and, in February 1932, she sailed under her own steam to Alloa for breaking up.

The Ayrshire Post published a nice little appreciation, almost an obituary, complete with photograph - "The Passing of the Juno".

T.S. DUCHESS OF HAMILTON (1932)

Juno was sadly missed, but she had a distinguished successor in the new turbine steamer, which cruised from Ayr until the outbreak of war in 1939.

T.S. DUCHESS OF MONTROSE (1930)

She cruised regularly down-firth to Ayr in the 1930's.

ABRAHAM RYDBERG

A Swedish barque from Stockholm, then a sail-training ship, at the Compass Pier in June 1937. (The late Alec Wills, who became Docks Foreman, always insisted that he was the boy on the right, playing on the slip!)

The ship had been built on the Clyde in 1892, by Charles Connell & Co. for American owners. She had an excellent record and, in 1937 and 1938, was the first ship home in the Grain Race from Australia to Britain.

On this occasion she had discharged wheat at Barrow, then came to Ayr to load coal and sailed for Mälmo.

MARCHIONESS OF GRAHAM (1936)

This pleasant little turbine steamer revived the Ayr excursion sailings after the war, from 1947 to 1953.

A Valentine postcard with *Marchioness of Graham* getting up steam on the south side of river, and *Lairdscrest* of the Burns Laird Line on the north quay wall.

The Ayrshire Post, January 1, 1954

There had been strong rumours that *Marchioness of Graham* was being withdrawn from Ayr, and the paper was doing its bit in the campaign to retain the excursion sailings. The ship was in fact withdrawn, but *Caledonia* carried out a modified programme of cruises in 1954.

THE AYRSHIRE POST, JANUARY 1, 1954

THOSE WERE THE DAYS

Damage to the Railway Bridge

In a severe storm in March 1949 *Cornish Coast* a ship being refitted in the shipyard, broke loose from her moorings and was blown violently against the bridge. She carried away one of the stone butts which can just be seen in the water.

The Shipyard in 1950 from the air

The yard had closed during the depression in 1929, but it was re-opened in 1941 by the London Graving Dock Co., on behalf of the Admiralty Merchant Shipbuilding and Repair Department. During the next two and a half years the incredible total of 670 vessels were repaired. Control then passed on to the Naval side of the Admiralty and after the war, in 1947, the yard was taken over by the Ayr Engineering and Constructional Co. Ltd..

This photo was taken from an excellent booklet "Contributions to Scottish Maritime History" by John Crighton Jnr. of that company. On the slip is *Queen Mary II* and a small tanker, *Shellbrit IX*; in the river are *Glen Sannox* and *Duchess of Hamilton*.

(The white line defines the limits of the shipyard.)

The slip dock, at the end of the prom, with *Duchess of Hamilton and Marchioness of Graham* in 1951.

P.S. CALEDONIA (1934)

The Ayr steamer from 1954 to 1964, berthed in the north harbour. She was an excellent solidly built ship from Denny of Dumbarton, and was designed for all-year round service. She also had two boilers, and if there were problems with one she could still proceed, albeit at reduced speed. Just astern of *Caledonia* is the steam dredger, *Carrick*.

DUCHESS OF HAMILTON

Duchess of Hamilton returned to the Ayr cruising scene from 1965 to 1969 but only for a Friday afternoon cruise round Holy Isle. She was taken out of service after the 1970 season.

Great efforts were made to try to save this fine ship, possibly as a floating restaurant in one of the Glasgow docks, but all the plans came to nothing.

Demise of the Duchess

Duchess of Hamilton was broken up at Troon, by the West of Scotland Shipbreaking Company in April, 1974.

KAFFIR

She was a traditional Clyde Puffer although she had been converted to a motor ship. Here she is aground off the Newton Shore in 1974.
It seems that an inebriated crew member took the vessel out of the harbour on his own; on the return journey he missed the harbour entrance.

Thirty years later, at low water much of the puffer is still visible.

P.S. WAVERLEY (1947)

Entering Ayr in style in 1975

When the ship was handed over to the Paddle Steamer Preservation Society by Caledonian MacBrayne, it was agreed that she would not use Gourock. She therefore concentrated on Glasgow at weekends and Ayr through the week.

South Harbour Street on a summer Monday afternoon.

The explanation. Waverley is about to leave for the popular cruise to Girvan and round Ailsa Craig.

WAVERLEY
Off the Compass Pier.

The ship is owned by a Registered Charity, Waverley Steam Navigation Company, and although in her six month season she travels nationwide, she sails out of Ayr regularly from the end of June until the end of August.

GARNOCK
The Irvine Harbour Tug

This beautifully maintained vessel occasionally helped in Ayr with very large ships. Here she is spick and span as usual in 1977. Unfortunately she is no longer active; she was dumping old explosives for I.C.I. (Ardeer) off Ailsa Craig in 1984, and one drum instead of sinking floated round under the stern. When the propellers started to rotate there was a massive explosion severely damaging the after end of the vessel. She was towed back to Troon where dry-docking proved it would have been uneconomic to restore her to active service. She is now at the Scottish Maritime Museum in Irvine.

However, what was on the other end of that tow-rope?

HAND FORTUNE

At 11,000 tons deadweight she was the largest ship to have entered Ayr harbour, and remains so. The limiting factor is the depth of water available which is 6.2 metres.

The Railway Bridge of 1899, over to the South Harbour, just before its demolition in 1978; the masonry butts were left in place. The white buildings on the north are on the site of the original Ayr railway station.

The Harbour framed by the Railway Bridge.

Pack Ice in the harbour in January 1982.

Russian Timber Ship in the ice. No doubt they'd feel very much at home.

PROOF GALLANT

This United States whisky tanker, made regular calls for the export of bulk whisky from Grant's Ladyburn Distillery at Girvan. Ladyburn then (1986) was said to be the biggest producer of Scotch Whisky.

SKEIDSFOSS

An Icelandic ship, bringing in seaweed meal for the alginate factory at Girvan.

Kelly's Coal Boat BALLYKERN and tug CERES

This family firm started in Belfast about 1836 and their first ship was bought in 1861. From the 1870's they regularly carried coal from Ayrshire to Northern Ireland, a trade which initially started about 1500. Sadly, after 120 years, John Kelly Ltd., disappeared from the scene in 1990.

Ballykern gained some notoriety in 1986 at the Old Bailey Trial of Patrick Magee, the Brighton bomber, and his four IRA Hit Squad members. It was mentioned that one of the gang was found to have a note with the words "Paddy, Ayr, the Ship Pub, Ballykern".

It seemed that Peter Sherry crossed from Belfast to Ayr on *Ballykern* and he then visited the Ship Inn in the North Harbour. Later he travelled on the "Paddy" (the Stranraer Boat Train), from Ayr to Carlisle where he met Patrick Magee.

It was really Sherry's arrival in Britain, through Ayr, that led to the break-up of the whole IRA cell.

THE MARINE BAR

This popular hostelry in South Harbour Street had an impressive horse-shoe Spanish mahogany panelled bar, and had been in the hands of the Calder family for three generations, since 1902.

When the area was being re-developed attempts were made to have it preserved, but it was demolished in 1992. The mahogany bar was transferred to the Market Inn.

Stained glass from the door of the Marine Bar showing an old paddle steamer.

PROBA

Unloading a cargo of Rock Salt, from Kilroot in Northern Ireland, to be used for gritting roads in winter.

A fine nautical gravestone for a sea captain, in Ayr Cemetery.

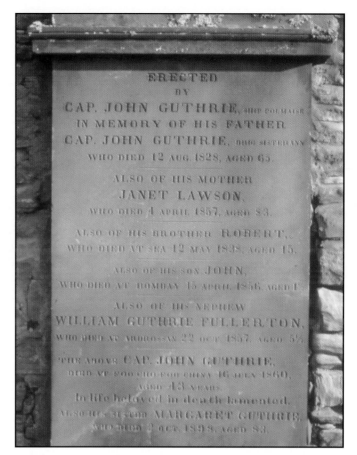

ERECTED
BY
CAP. JOHN GUTHRIE, SHIP POLMAISE
IN MEMORY OF HIS FATHER
CAP. JOHN GUTHRIE, BRIG SISTER ANN
WHO DIED 12 AUG. 1828, AGED 65.

ALSO OF HIS MOTHER
JANET LAWSON,
WHO DIED 4 APRIL 1857, AGED 83.

ALSO OF HIS BROTHER ROBERT,
WHO DIED AT SEA 12 MAY 1828, AGED 15.

ALSO OF HIS SON JOHN,
WHO DIED AT BOMBAY 15 APRIL 1856, AGED 1½.

ALSO OF HIS NEPHEW
WILLIAM GUTHRIE FULLERTON,
WHO DIED AT ARDROSSAN 22 OCT. 1857, AGED 5½.

THE ABOVE CAP. JOHN GUTHRIE,
DIED AT FOO-CHO-FOO CHINA 16 JULY 1860,
AGED 43 YEARS.
In life beloved in death lamented.
ALSO HIS SISTER MARGARET GUTHRIE,
WHO DIED 2 OCT. 1898, AGED 83.

Newton Green Cemetery

There are numerous stones here of maritime interest, as the ship-masters tended to live north of the river. This stone was erected by Capt. John Guthrie, Ship *Polmaise*, in memory of his father, also Capt. John, Brig *Sister Ann*, who died in 1828.

What follows below is a rather depressing social commentary eg. his brother died at sea aged 15, his son died at Bombay aged 1½ and his nephew died at Ardrossan aged 5½. Captain Guthrie himself died at Foo-Cho-Foo, China, aged 43 years.

Well that's how it was, at least for one sex; two of the ladies mentioned reached 83 years.

The Fishermen's Dock
(Between the white and red flats)

After the Battle of Bannockburn in 1314, King Robert the Bruce nominated 48 Freemen of Newton - on - Ayr as a reward for valour, and gave each a portion of land called a Freedom. The title "Freeman" was hereditary but seemed to be marketable, and one of a Freeman's rights was that in this part of the harbour, his fishing boat could lie free of all charges.

The system lapsed when Newton ceased to be a separate burgh but, even up to 25 years ago, there were rumours around the harbour about someone, Tam Toner, who claimed to be the last of the Freemen.

Enquiries at the usual sources of local information drew a blank, and the story was dismissed as the kind of thing circulated in the pubs. Sure enough a visit to what was then Graham's Bar in Main Street produced a friendly welcome and the answer.

THOMAS TONER

(BIG TAM)

A RESIDENT OF AYR HARBOUR AREA

FROM 1915 TO 1981

A light went out in the Harbour,

The night Tam Tonner died,

His body you ken, lay in his ben

While his soul went out on the tide.

Tam Toner at the Fishermen's Dock

Photo and Plaque, from Graham's Bar. So he was real flesh and blood after all and had been an engine driver at the harbour. He kept a boat and, while I doubt if officially he was granted free moorings on the strength of his claim to be the last Freeman, the Chief Clerk of that time had no recollection of him paying anything.

The Auld Kirk

This was built in 1654 as a replacement for the Church of St. John the Baptist at the Fort, which had been taken over by Cromwell's troops and used as an Armoury. The original model which was placed here above the Sailors' Loft, was presented in 1662 by the crew of a French barque, which had been wrecked in Ayr Bay, in thanks for their deliverance and in gratitude for hospitality received.

By 1802 it had deteriorated and was replaced by this model, "*Arethusa*". Also shown are the Colours of the Royal North British Fusiliers and (bottom left) the statuette of Robert Burns.

The North Harbour in a heat wave in July 1984. In fact this was a plastic mock-up for the making of a T.V. film "The Last Place on Earth", featuring Martin Shaw, about Scott's last expedition.

This ship *Kaskelot,* became both Scott's *Terra Nova* with dummy funnel and deckhouse, complete with huskies, ponies and pemmican, and later Amundsen's *Fram.*

Dunure became Quail Island, off New Zealand, from which Scott made his departure. Note *Terra Nova* at sea.

Rebuilding the Compass Pier, 1986

At one stage it seemed possible that the crumbling pier would never be rebuilt, which would have been a major problem for *P.S. Waverley*. However, eventually the work went ahead. Just behind the pier on the right is the Yacht Club, and the light building on its left is the Fishermen's Mission.

The Lighthouse, North Harbour

This was built by Robert Paton in 1843, and initially the illumination was provided by an oil lamp. The cottage was added in 1850 and a family lived there until at least 1957. This is one of the leading lights for shipping approaching the harbour and provides the red landward light.

The photograph was taken in 1992, after renovation of the the lighthouse by the Scottish Maritime Museum.

An unusual import - steel wire coils from Lisbon.

An unusual export - *Igloo Sky* took refrigerated meat to Egypt.

Ashington, London, fitted with the Walker Wingsail in 1986. This invention from a Southampton firm, was said to save 10% of the fuel costs of this bulk carrier.

Ashington again two years later, when the apparatus seemed to have developed. However it can't have been a great success as the last time the vessel was in Ayr, the Wingsail had been removed.

Northern Boundary of the Port of Ayr

The extent of various ports was accurately defined for Customs and Excise purposes; in the case of Ayr this was done in 1830 and this stone is in Troon, off South Beach, at Craigend Burn one mile south of Troon Point.

Southern Boundary of the Port of Ayr

This is at Carleton Bay, just south of Lendalfoot; the stone was recently moved a little in the course of road re-alignment.

The boundary line then goes west-ward to Ailsa Craig, thence to Pladda at the southern point of Arran, and finally back to the stone in Troon.

Patziel of Vienna, with a cargo of Dolomite Sand from Malaga. Most of the harbour got covered by this material.

Another dusty cargo - Soda Ash from Garston for glass-making at Rockware, Irvine.

Partial damming of the river, at the butts of the old railway bridge. A central gap was left to produce a more vigorous flow there, in the hope that less dredging would be required. However this did not produce the benefit that had been expected.

Sylvia MacAlpine feeding the harbour swans around 4pm, as she has done for years, just upstream of the Auld Brig. The food came from ASDA but, now that the store has moved it is hoped there will be no interruption in the supply.

"Buttons" the Goose

Ayr's Sea-going Swans

The Slip at the Compass Pier

In 1991 he decided to join the flotilla of 80 swans, and there was much discussion about what type of goose he was. Eventually Angus Hogg, the local expert, pronounced that he was an ordinary farmyard goose; he had had his wings clipped, couldn't fly, and had probably been washed down the river, from somewhere like Muirkirk, in a spate.

This is not used much for small boats nowadays, but a swan's nest doesn't make it any easier.

Looking upstream from the butts of the old railway bridge to the High Flats of Riverside Place.

Looking downstream from the High Flats.

Not a particularly suitable berth for *Waverley,* but scrap metal is a major export, much of it going to Spain through Henderson and Kerr.

A Seaplane with two Americans on a Round-the-World trip, in aid of the Special Olympics in 1990. They had called in at Ayr for repairs.

SEISMARINER

A Norwegian seismographic ship in Ayr in 1992. She had been surveying for oil between Ailsa Craig and Northern Ireland. Small explosions are used and the reflected shock waves are studied; there are two miles of cable and varying the length used gives different profile views of the strata.

Cave Sand of Grimsby dredging in 1993. The Monkey Jetty is prominent in the foreground.

The demolition of Ayr Yacht Club in 1994. A sad sight, indeed.

Old Milestone preserved by the demolishers. It had been incorporated in the southernmost gatepost of the Yacht Club compound (previously the main gate of McKnight's Shipyard). Inscribed on the right face was "Maybole by Alloway Bridge 7^1/$_2$ miles", on the left face "Maybole by Monkwood Bridge 8 miles" and, on the top surface "Ayr 1 mile". Obviously it must have come from the gushet at St. Leonard's Church and this was confirmed by the Ordnance Survey map of 1856.

Ground for St. Leonard's (1886) would have been cleared around the time the shipyard moved to the south harbour, in 1883. But why was the stone moved down to the gatepost there? The Parks Department were very helpful and the stone has been returned to St. Leonard's.

ARKLOW MEADOW

Laden with coal for Eire, in 1994.

George Wylie's Paper Boat *Queen Mary*. A contribution to the 1994 Arts Festival, to remind us of what once we could do on the Clyde.

The Fishing Fleet in 1989

Mending the Nets, with the Ice Factory above.

Harvest Home

"Memorial to a Dying Industry"

George Wylie's symbolic fish at the 1995 Arts Festival.

"Reminiscence"

This fine statue by Malcolm Robertson, at the Fish Cross, cannot compensate for the sad loss of the reduced fishing fleet to Troon, after almost 800 years. The move took place in 1996.

Miller's Folly (one careful owner!)

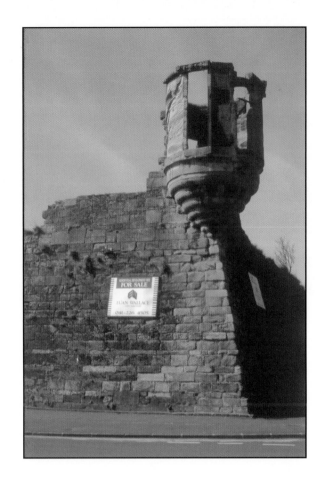

The "For Sale" notices were attached by an over-enthusiastic advertising agent and referred to the adjacent Citadel Development.

The Fort area was purchased in 1853 by John Watson Miller, from the Kennedys. Miller was an eccentric gunsmith and antiquarian who had made a fortune in Calcutta; he converted the Tower of St. John into a Gothic-style Fort Castle residence, where he lived as Baron Miller till he died in 1910.

He apparently built the Folly with his own hands, on the corner of Cromwell's Fort, in the second part of the 19th Century.

The old Custom House in Fort Street, opposite Ayr Academy, was built c. 1810 and is now a Listed Building.

M.V. EXPLORER

Chartered by SAGA, in Ayr in August 1996. She was one of the early cruise ship visitors, and originally was meant to visit Londonderry. However anticipated trouble with the Apprentice Boys' March caused a change of plan.

SAINT KEARAN

J & A Gardner's chemical tanker had brought in Calcium Chloride for the Alginate Factory at Dipple, Girvan, from Winnington, Liverpool.

A Drilling Barge checking the river bed to allow fixation of a pontoon for small yachts, in 1998.

The towing boat is *Kingfisher*, used by Tony Medina over many years to provide fishing trips.

PAPHOS

After almost 500 years of the export of coal from Ayr, in 1998 this vessel is bringing coal into Ayr, from Colombia. Small amounts of high quality coal also came in from China and Russia.

GUARDSMAN

This rig tender was operating west of Ireland, during the summer of 1998. Enterprise Oil was opening up a gas field but there was some difficulty with the trade unions, and the company decided to base its rig tenders in Ayr.

The new cruise liner, *Norwegian Dream,* off Ayr, April 1999. She has accommodation for 1,700 passengers.

NORWEGIAN DREAM and WAVERLEY off AYR

NORWEGIAN SKY

Off Ayr in July 1999. She was a new ship of Norwegian Cruise Lines capable of carrying 2,000 passengers. This photograph was taken from The Mount and St Leonard's Church is seen on the right.

ROYAL VIKING SUN

Off Ayr in September 1999, a Cunard liner of around 80,000 tons.

A new sewer had to be laid under the river in 2000 and these pipes are awaiting installation.

This was the storm overflow for the Barassie sewer.

The Jack-up Rig awaiting action, in the Griffen Dock.

Cruise Ship *M.V. Bremen*, leaving Ayr in June 2000.

White Sand from Lochaline being unloaded for glass-making at Rockware, Irvine.

HMS Sandown, a Mine Hunter. There are occasional visits from Customs, Fishery, and small Naval Vessels.

Proxigean (Negative) Tide 8th May 2001, taken from the South Harbour looking upstream.
When the Moon is closest to the Earth, but on the opposite side from the Sun, during Full Moon it produces unusually low neap tides.

Red Baroness owned by Robin Taylor of Troon brings in timber from Ardrishaig, Campbeltown and Sandbank on the Holy Loch. It goes to the Caledonian Paper Mills at Meadowhead, Irvine.

This timber from Arran came in by barge towed by a tug from Troon, again Taylor's.

Timber awaiting shipment.

BREMER SATURN

This large ship is bound for Halle, Finland with Scottish timber from Galloway. The successful use of our logs, for paper making at Irvine, led to the development of this export trade.

The rectangular structure amidships on the port side is a loading ramp.

ARCHANGEL VISITOR

МЕХАНИК СЕМАКОВ in 2003 brought in machined timber from Onega.

МЕХАНИК ТIOAEHEB, a sister Russian ship on the same run.

Kyle, the Pilot Boat.

Head to Head

On the left *Nevag,* of Farsund, Norway, had brought sand from Lochaline for Rockware.
On the right *Silver Stream* of Grimsby had been fishing in the Atlantic.

A busy harbour in June 2003

The red ship is *Saltstraum* of Bergen, which had brought in Calcium Chloride for the Alginate Factory at Girvan. Beyond her is *Hebridean Princess* (previously MacBrayne's *Columba*); she is now a small select cruise ship carrying only 38 passengers. In the foreground is the yacht pontoon.

Red Baroness loading fertiliser (Dunn's Soil Fertility have a base in the harbour). In the spring, this is delivered to Islay, Campbeltown and Bute.

Pamir (Haren-Ems) unloading salt for Messers. Peacock, North Harbour.

Sommen (Karlstad) entering Ayr on 9th November 2004 for a cargo of timber; she was the second largest ship to have entered the port.

Regine bringing Windfarm equipment into Ayr at the end of May 2005.

This equipment had come from Denmark and it was bound for Hadyard Hill near Barr in South Ayrshire. It could not be moved outwith the harbour area until after 8pm and required a police escort.

These are segments of columns but there were also cone-shaped turbines.

Regine partly unloaded. Incidentally this picture illustrates well the ship's modern bulbous bow.

The Bridge over what was the slip-dock at the end of the prom. This is in roughly the same position as Provost Thomas Steele's Swing Bridge. The old Coastguard Tower is clearly seen.

The stone platform in front of the tower previously accommodated these cannons, known as The Battery.

The Chart Reference for the Port of Ayr is just opposite the Tower, facing east.

LOYAL WATCHER

This vessel from Plymouth visits Ayr in the summer and takes parties of divers out as far as Malin Head. Apparently they can descend to 90 metres.

The South Pier

Red Baroness leaving

Evening Peace

From the Fishermen's Dock

Alastair MacFarlane

Port Manager
Associated British Ports

Captain Newton Brown

Previous Harbour Master
In his retirement
Relief Master of *Red Baroness*

Philip Lilley

Present Harbour Master